FM GHOST

Steve Shultz

ISBN: 978-0615799971

ALL CAPS PUBLISHING

Cover photo/design by Steve Shultz

Author photo by Melinda Shultz

ALL CAPS PUBLISHING

P.O. Box 368, Easthampton, MA 01027

allcapspublishing.com

For Melinda,
my favorite.

CONTENTS

WITHIN:

WITHOUT:

WITHIN:

WITHIN

FM GHOST

Wish I had a radio voice.

But these words weren't meant to soothe.
Simply stated, they need to be said.
They need to be freed,
like a wrongly-accused poltergeist.

I am not
the smooth sounds of now,
climbing up the charts
of syrupy saccharine
candy cane rungs.

I am
a work in progress.

I am
rough around the edges of an incomplete circle.

I am
beautifully flawed,
like a butterfly in the mouth of a predator.

I am.
Like it, or not.

And I need to free this ghost from mind.

20 YEARS

For twenty years I've lived with you,
or rather you inside me.

Needle pricks through hardened skin,
into fat and on through blood.

Saving me with immediacy
as long term takes a toll.

Needing more, my bones ache.
Body breaks down from inside out.

For twenty years I've fought you.
Will there be twenty more?
I want to watch my children grow.

Who wins this medicated death dance?
Elevator goes up, goes down.
I await the certainty of cables snapping.

Who is this repo man?
Eager for the harvest
after flesh and blood shut down,

sifting spirit through a sieve
of blackened past.

Twenty years is a long time;
calloused fingers no longer feel pain.

I want to tell that boy of ten,
who was so afraid of needles:
You get used to the sting.

PITCH BLACK

I watch her chest rise and fall
just like the sun's daily regimen.
it happens so much faster than
watching leaves fall and grow anew next spring.
still, I anticipate each next breath
as if it won't arrive.
as if tomorrow the sun would not rise.

as if this mine cart would just keep climbing
on its own momentum, never falling.
forcing butterflies to flee
from stomach's bile on up through throat.
as if opposites refused to exist.

I watch the laugh lines form on her face
and anticipate tears to salt rosy cheeks.
I see a glass and I measure it empty in quarters
because I know that birth must soon mean death.

yet along the way I forgot how to live.
and if we're not living
then we can only be one thing.

because gray is not a color,
but it is how my heart feels:
hollow to the marrow.
stumbling over simple subtraction.

some say there is light in death,
and it must be so because life is dark.

AWAKEN RAYS

Bony ribs allude
creamy skin
curly locks of golden
rays, purest sunshine

duck lips
eyes of the finest
furniture brown

in this moment
I know exactly
what life's about

sweet voice
I savor every broken syllable
of her 2-year-old speech

her little
less-than 30-lb self
heavier, my heart
on days without

LONG TIME, NO SHIVA

It was a month
of drunken show and tell.
Who's got the best toy,
who's got the biggest
tale to yell.

Never too old for this mirror.
Rub eyes to see reflection pooled.
Here again, in this pagan pantheon,
poisoned by the contents
of Shiva's medicine cabinet.

Maybe next month will be different.

SELF-MADE

I rule
I survey
I stop the train
when running late
I destroy
when unable to create

AFFECTATION

Give and take
meet me in the middle
patiently wait
to board the ferry

Bare hands shake
never to meet again
knuckles scrape
across familiar faces

Who is at the helm
that I am so underwhelmed
so vehemently defeated
pasts destined to repeat

Who is at the door
rejected, once adored
directionally misguided
truths cleverly disguised

Who comes through but you
independently divided
severely disconnected
true interest affected

Who is watching guard
that we go by undetected
easily ignored
swept under rug

Old hands break
crippled and palsied
knuckles taped
to work for one more day

Give and take
meet me on the last nerve
patiently wait
to sever synapses

SWITCH

Switch goes on/off,
watch the fan blades
slow to a stop.

on/off/on/off/on
and off again.

in control,
a child
who can't stop playing
with power windows.

off/on/off/on/off
and on again.

plus or minus,
it does not matter;
we are just motors
waiting to burn out.

LOSING ST. CHRISTOPHER

I once had a Saint Christopher medal
A reminder of faith and believing
Gone like the color from fallen petals
I lost my protection one fall evening
Season of innocence changed to grieving
My angel at bottom of a leaf pile
On ground desperately searching for meaning
Somehow watched over mile by mile

GAIA TREE

This tree,
it made you and me.
gave birth to life
and lost its leaves
each season.

weathering standstill,
this oak tree's
knuckled limbs
lifted up the world.

my Mother,
I owe you everything
and can repay
not one single strip of bark.

it tears me up inside,
why hands you've worked to bone
won't heal.

we just age and age
and shed our skin
upon this barren sand.

this tree provides sustenance,
we suck Her dry
and pray for rain.

Mother,
how can I make it right?
but do right by
my own seedlings.

they will know
kindness,
nonviolence,
and everything of which
this world we live.

I will do right
by you and them,
and everyone who's ever
shed a tear

for what I fear tears me up inside.

THE WEEK OF DANCERS & DREAMERS

He was born in the week
of dancers and dreamers
Stars all aligned for him
to be a great thinker

A little late for
the week of the loner
The great wheel at last
has come full circle

He spreads his wings, he is destined for great things

A wanderlust
A Pisces fish
swimming upstream
in Neptune's waters

Some find him strange
Some find him peculiar
He makes unbelievable possible
and impossible believable

He can see both sides of a one-sided story

Last of all signs
Last of all cycles
Shadows on the sundial
have come full circle

He's a miracle maker
A bread baker
He's got a hand to lend
and an open ear

No time for apathy
No need for sympathy
Eyes wide, his heart beats empathy

Me, I'm the enigma, and my father's a child

DEEP END ANT

I am an ant drowning
in the deep end of creation

don't want to be buried
alive, so I settle
for waterfront cremation

inching to one day snap
these puppet strings

itching to one day break
this hold you got on me

I can pull my weight, but
can't outrun this sadistic
schoolboy's magnifying glass

I am a beetle on its back
about to be washed down drain

I am a turtle stripped of shell
pawned for a softer spot in hardened heart

I am an old soul
been around this old block
but I can't seem to blow this ant hole

MEMOIRS

Frail and fatigued
this body
hanging on to

roadshow antiques
judged by experts
of currency

to shining things
that rust
in box, in god

we trust
ashes and dust
to become

memoirs
in an armoire
that no one shall read

EATER OF WORLDS

He draws
stick figures
with such passion

with flick of wrist
he sets into being
imperfect circles
disproportionate limbs

eyes larger than life
mouth a single line
defying
happy sad
anger resolve

a mad man outlined
in orange marker
eats dots
tiny worlds
revolve round 2-D self

finger's cocked
he's shooting
satellite moons

in scribbled spirals
he scribes
dreams on white sheets

rainbow's array to choose from
his mind's the limit
transcending sky's varied sunsets

before the paint dries
with surest certainty
he moves on to the next world

CLIPPED WINGS

I miss you
but I'm not
yet ready to be home

been away far
too long but not
yet ready to return

forgetting fixtures
just miles away
origin unattainable

I want to be
on that stage
taking breath away

why angels choose
to clip own wings and fall...
wonder why life's flightless

sharing split seconds
and hoping for minutes
cannot fly free from spiderweb

REPLACEMENT PARTS

Is there any respite
for tired bones?
a brittle impermanence

a residence of
hospice once a home
never writing letters

never sending word
that all is well
all is swollen

in need of ice bag
salt bath to soak
these mired bones

replace bad parts
with spark
no more workarounds

ah, but we would grow
so bored not dying
laugh through the pain

laugh all the same
all cut from cloth
but we do not laugh the same

CLAUSTROPHOBIC TIME TRAVELER

Claustrophobic dreams
thoughts constrict
around my windpipe
small-minded people
trapped in small places

walls dark and damp
breathing restricted
this is no way to travel
panic is setting in
underneath my suit

I can't breathe
I can't fit
in this tiny space
but it's the only way
the only way to get to you

I can't reach
I can't move
in this crowded elevator...

f
a
l
l
i
n
g

...but it's the only way to get to you

there is no glass to break
there is no emergency exit
the only way to you
the only way through is fear

I can't find the light switch
there is no panic button
so I will hold my breath
and drop up into this mystery abyss

CELL

Every seven years
change shape
change stride

Who am I?
I am not that boy
Who are you?
I am not that boy
and you are not that man

regenerate
rejuvenate
pass home plate
degenerate

it's all downhill
from here

see you in another
multiple of seven
if I'm still able
to recognize that face

ASCENDING

This hole knows my name
its whispers wind
through cavern's conclaves
terrestrial tinnitus

this hole knows my depth
I dug it myself
grain by grain
with rusted spade

this hole counts my days
it knows my hate
it is my pain
but it does not know my fate

regained the strength
to jump out of the shade
today's the day
I climb out of this cave

found my spade, patiently
pack that fucker with dirt
and wash myself clean
in the surety of sunshine

CROCUSES & DAFFODILS

Antsy for this snow to melt

she's counting
the days till
spring appears

counting the days
on little paper rings

colors of Easter
only 24 more
to rip down

crocuses & daffodils
poking through the mud

my son is turning 5 this year

bedroom's white walls
still need painted

finally going to plant that garden

CLOCKWISE

These bones, receptors
reservoirs of pain

these parts, not meant
to be overloaded with joy

these hands,
pain moves clockwise
always perfect time

we walk on splintered marrow
in hopes of better tomorrow

these nerves are shot
patience numbed
symptoms abbreviated

there is no cheese
only dangled carrot

who's winning this race
of donkeys, beasts of burden?

tell me, for what
tell me why we savor blood

SILENT SIREN

She is my favorite
flavor
when everyone
is so goddamn vanilla

she's like a breath
of fresh air
when I'm rummaging
head down in the dumps

a sigh of relief when
my very soul is dislocated
soon to be set
by a black-market dentist

this idle ambulance
disturbs me
much more than
the siren

tell me now
is it my time to die
would I really live this day
any different from the rest

spare my feelings
strangle emotions
straight the face
of death's informant

maybe next time
we can have a drink
or two before the deal
before I drool off into eternity

maybe next time
I'll listen
before the silent siren
ushers us into static

ONE HALLOWEEN

One Halloween, I didn't dress up.
Got my face painted with real blood.

It was 2 a.m. and I told the wrong
person to turn the stereo down.

One Halloween, I played pretend.
My costume, self-importance.

Anger, head-butted in bridge of nose.
Adrenaline cushioned further blows.

One Halloween, I didn't fight back;
me, a frozen caricature at bottom of stairs.

I retreated, grabbed my switchblade.
Stuffed it in my pocket to feel safe.

Did I really think I'd pull it out?
Then what, draw blood?

One Halloween ruined many after.
It was the season I should have hit back.

GRANDMA'S SPARE BED

I miss sleeping
in Grandma's spare bed

the pillows were so firm
on Grandma's spare bed

now Grandma is gone
and so's her spare bed

sometimes I smell her perfume
and see her in dreams

but my head rests no more
on Grandma's spare bed

SONRISE

He wants to fly planes
put out fires
save lives
conduct trains

he wants to operate
heavy machinery
smash cars
with heavy things

Where did my ambition go?
Passed down through the ages

He has my eyes —
no, that's a lie
his are much
brighter than mine

He has my face —
no, that's untrue
his is much softer
and brighter, too

He came from me
and her and seeds
we never even knew

seeds that grew
from yesterdays
to shape a future, bright
when my own self-doubt puts lights out

at least a part of me
can dream, achieve, believe

He makes me smile
when surrounded
by a crowd of frowns

He makes me laugh
when the world's
dressed for a funeral

He is a ball of brilliant light
in the darkest corners of my mind
from the ashes I watch him rise

THIS KISS

Like Paris
I'm feeling plastered
it never looks as good
as it does in the movies

still, hold me
till the credits roll

Apatow's got
nothing on our gag reel
this is real
do you feel it?

hold me
till the credits roll

wrap me up in
your letters & numbers
lose me
in your white on black

just one more shot
give me credit
for this kiss

BEACHED

You left me
here
on this
god-forsaken beach

I wanted to taste
the salty air
of freedom, found
lifeline trapped
in every pebble
each hermit crab

ate up all the fish and fruit
water's run dry
in the sand I drew this heart
in hopes you'd see
it beat, profess
my remorse

deus ex machina
come down, sweep me off my feet
and tell me
it was my choice all along

ask me
will I do it all over again

SWALLOW

Where would we be
if it weren't
for death and birth

lessons learned
blank pages,
god it hurts

how many times
must we fail this course
the questions look different
but the test is the same

how many times
must we sharpen
pencil stubs

Where would we be
if it weren't
for death/rebirth

in this current
go-round the ocean
will I sink, or will I swim

will we meet again
when the gates open up
and we're swallowed
by our actions/reactions

how many times
must we choose
water over air

god it hurts to swallow

MUTE

We share the same bed
when in dreams we are so distant

my greatest nightmare
is being stifled
unable

to communicate

attacker's hands
close around my throat
crushing my breath

I can't speak up
I can't overpower

I am frozen
consumed by an unseen monster

faceless attacker
just a head of hair, skin
blurred smooth, no features

hands squeeze tight around my throat

I have a gun
I pull the trigger
the gun won't fire

throwing punches
fists are sandbags
sinking weight
in swimming pool

hands around my throat
not hairy, clawed
or even of a stranger

these hands are fear
these hands are mine

COLOR BY NUMBERS

Painting your picture, I lose violent hues,
look through your window to choose vibrant views.
At peace! At peace! To one day be,
with your world and internally.
Color by numbers, your canvas too white;
the end result blinds, its face is too bright.

Composing a hymn you might like to hear;
at peace with myself, true thought disappears.
Be free! Be free! To truly be,
from your world I may one day see.
Hands grasping at straws for all the right words;
be free, these words, to your window like birds.

WITHIN MINUTES

One dies.
One is born.

Out with cardiac arrest;
breathing in through new lungs.

How to keep these insides vital.
How to walk with purpose in mind.

Why are we alive?
Too many distractions,
too little time.

Why get sick and die.
Too many attachments,
too little time.

One is born.
One dies.

Out with open eyes;
in with blinding light.

Now to keep these insides vital.
Now to walk with purpose in mind.

ALL POINTS BETWEEN

I need an idea.
One that won't wilt,
wither and die.
From malnutrition,
cynicism
or just plain boredom.

I need a spark.
To kindle a flame.
To start a fire
that will burn clean.
Leave no ashes,
no trace of smoke.

I need to make a dent
in this tin can.
To scratch the surface,
to not feel worthless.
A sharpened tool
for a weakened trade.

I need to break through
to something true.
To any side,
many corners.
Collapse this box.
Shatter ceilings.

What I don't need
is stumbling blocks.
Fumbling talk.
Stupid answers
to pointless questions,
not worth a breath.

What I could use,
a clever ruse.
Fruit not bruised,
not rotting mold.
Stories of old,
rightly told.

I sure don't need
you in the way.
Misdirecting traffic
on a road mispaved.
A stick in the spokes,
a rake in the face.

I really could use
a stunning debut.
A glorious exit, but...
What really matters
is all points between,
who I need to be.

ROCK CHANDELIER

Today
I am outweighed
By anchors ripping clouds
By upstanding conveyances
Sky bound

Today
No more dismay
No more adjectives for
falling airplanes and poking at
bruises

Outweighed
Happy to say
The sky is the limit
Willing to break rock chandelier
with fall

Outweighed
By things do change
For the better if I
grab the wheel and steer this vessel
off rocks

Today
will be that day
I'm taking back the reins
I'm melting icebergs, removing
roadblocks

Today
No more dismay
The sky is the limit
Grab the reins and steer this vessel
sky bound

WITHOUT

FAT BIRDS

Stale pieces of bread and bird shit
litter the walkway.

We live in a society
where most people feed pigeons
but not the homeless.

Is that all we are to become?
Concrete stains?
Skin & bones. And the birds are fat.

Both dirty, disease ridden.
Both pariahs, leaving dregs behind.
One is plump, the other skinny.

And the birds are fat. And getting fatter.
On stale bread crumbs & spilled cereal.

Brown-bagging my way up
the corporate ladder, stuck on low rung.
I walk on by the birds & the homeless,
spitting my disgust upon the sidewalk.

What are we to become
but concrete stains.
Skin & bones, and the birds are fat.

PASSING JUDGMENT

Every time I pass by the corner of Clarkson and 13th
I wonder why you have to hold that sign.
A tattered piece of cardboard
discarded from someone else's hot meal
or case of cold beer.

Probably you're trying to get a slice
of pizza from Benny Blanco's up the block,
or maybe a pint of Jack,
or vodka if you prefer.
A pack of smokes, or papers
for the grass you scrounged up.

Probably you're a junkie aching for a fix,
a dead spider web spilling from the center
of your arm, branching around the sides
like a failed tribal tattoo.
Probably you need to get a REAL job.

Likely looking for a handout, a freebie,
a piece of my American apple pie,
my spare change to buy the change
we were promised with an air of hope.
A taste of the fruits of MY labor.

And what of your brothers and sisters
on the corner of everywhere U.S.A.
Do you share the same hard times, goals,
aspirations, addictions and malnutrition
written in black marker, once fresh and bold?

Why are there so many of you on every corner
like a Starbucks closed for business?
Foreclosed on life to dive through dumpsters.
Rummaging through society's landfill
for proofs of the same cardboard cutouts.

Every time I'm on the corner of Clarkson and 13th
I pass judgment, avoid eye contact.
I keep walking, even if my shoes are untied.
I never stop to give you a dime or a light.
I never stop, but I do think "that could be me."

WING TIPS

Do angels stub their wing tips up on high?
Hung up on prayers and stuck in the clouds
A heathen grasps lantern of seraphim's light
Do angels stub their wing tips up on high?

Affectatious check watch, for end time's nigh
While stubborn attempt to unwrap death's shroud
Do angels stub their wing tips up on high?
Hung up on prayers and stuck in the clouds

THREADBARE

Fighting the urge inside hidden pocket
Who put it there, all threadbare
Keep my faith tucked in a half-heart locket
Fighting the urge inside hidden pocket

Stole my sight just to dust out the sockets
Need not eyes for soulful stare
Fighting the urge inside hidden pocket
Who put it there, all threadbare

THE POSTCARD

Postcard filled
with last-minute postscripts

an abbreviated addendum
to a failed communique

pretty cursive
flowery language
stamped from faraway

message received
remains unread

postcard returned
to sender, rejected
correspondence
strictly one way

DAMAGED, STARK

Nibbling on van Gogh's dead ear
Snuffed out, searching for a spark
Ghosts long gone still anchored near

Quiet, scared of who might hear
Grasping for straws in the dark
Nibbling on van Gogh's dead ear

Reflecting glass is oldest fear
Truthful image: damaged, stark
Ghosts long gone still anchored near

Cities drown in single tear
Reality rips like bark
Nibbling on van Gogh's dead ear

Past missteps now all so clear
Pay no mind, the angel's hark
Ghosts long gone still anchored near

Always rank life second tier
Embracing death on a lark
Nibbling on van Gogh's dead ear
Ghosts long gone still anchored near

BORROWED SYMBOLS

Nobody's side
nobody's son
ride the high, no
never tall enough one

sifting through sand
heavy, quick
to drag fool down
when grasping for gold

soft crown
head held under
murky water
born to be bloated

eyelids too heavy
to follow bright stars
big moons

sleep to dream
dark paths, rusted forks
in roads long dusted over

wish for
one hand beanstalk
other palm, thorn-full

choking on the truth
this meat never tasted
so good

dripping sentiments
ill-begotten gains
medium rare

before too much pulls you low
losing velocity on a stone's throw

gravity smirks & laughs
baptized in a sea of borrowed symbols

OVERTAKEN

She could not part with
departed hearts
on leave, her own was
one great depression
once flooded with tears
overtaken by drought

Who will stop this whirlwind
from eating its own tail?
Who will break this fallen figure 8

All takers overtaken
in what's come of past mistakes
There will be time for more
I promise you
There will always be time to stand still

To rectify
To course correct
Could you be more direct?
To set straight
this lightning bolt road
From A to Z
this alphabet is wrecked

But there will always be time to set it right
If you could only part with one more broken heart

ALL THE OTHER GIRLS

All the other girls
in the schoolyard
bring red balloons

she brings a zeppelin
tied to her finger
guides it around
like a well-behaved dog

swimming in the sky
those girls' balloons
won't fly so high

All the other girls
in the schoolyard
seem happy in their everyday-ness
(in their sameness)

she'll drag the sun down
in her discontent
her brilliant zeppelin
turned fiery debris

she has seen the truth
and would never trade her
heavy burden for a red balloon

BEHOLDINGS

Beauty is blind
seen through eye
of beholder

disfigured stick figure
in image of creator

beauty walks around
on hobbled legs
with cane

beauty is clutching
brown bag, concealing
self-sorcerer's stone

beauty is an orange peel
browned, discarded
on a hungry corner

beauty is dog shit
obstacles
on uneven sidewalks

beauty is outlined in white chalk

beauty is dirty city snow
that sits for months
filthy landlocked icebergs

beauty sparkles like glass
from shattered
passenger-side windows

beauty is the rain getting in

beauty is the hole
smashed console
where stereo once lived

beauty is backing
into pedestrians
as we speak

beauty is a lack of witness
and walking away
unscathed

beauty is karmic justice
transferring power
from one hand to the other

beauty is both
self-inflicted
& unconditional

beauty is not knowing when to stop

(INNER)

Who will play you in this adaptation?

Outside your inner circle,
hiding like a diagnosis.

Looking for what's always been
hanging in plain sight.

A placard noose;
a do not disturb sign,

sticking out like a toenail
broken from shoving foot in mouth.

Your tears: a lanyard for my soul.

VIGIL

to serve
and protect,
projectile
rubber bullet
fractures
peaceful skull
of U.S. vet.
spoon fed
rainbow colors
turn knots
in stomach,
sudden need
to projectile vomit.
conglomerate
coffee, bitter
alongside
daily news.

*** ***

lights are out,
hands tremble
as they feel
for a candle.

WHEREAS

Constitution is a body mutilated by age

Liberty, a limping leg
mangled in lawnmower blades of green-grass pursuits

Justice, a spine jackknifed
for straightening up to take the stand

Equality, a head severed
into symmetrical parts of original thought

Freedom, a liver failed
while drinking from life's spring

Women's rights, a womb hijacked
by religious artifacts

Peaceful protest, arms restrained,
fingers snap with good intentions

Life, a pacemaker
pumping rusted blood through varicose veins

Constitution is a body mutilated by age;
we the people hold out for a cure

HEAVY SKELETONS

these skeletons
weigh a ton
shadows fondle
neutron bomb

thoughts scatter
megatons
blocks of cinder
crushing sternum

take a walk in
walk-in closet
suits pressed
dressed dour

nooses tied
and loosened
assorted patterns
screws the past turns

breathe the dust
from archived microfibers

SCHOOLYARD SECRETS

Her kisses
shatter myths
rose quartz bricks
line schoolyard secrets
constructed from
top-shelf surplus.

SHURIKEN KISSES

She throws kisses like ninja stars
as she smiles from the shadows.
Like lobotomy, she cuts
the meaning from my words.
Defeated, my lips left wishing for *seppuku*.

HALLMARKED

A holy day is shelved,
for sale at supermarket
super mega store,
big-boxed
front window display

months before
calendar date
of said holiday

a holy day,
heavily discounted
on departmental pews,
diabetic premonitions
on exhibit

70% off
just one day
past expiration date

chocolate deity
gifts of jellybeans
in baskets of paper grass
eyes are dollar signs

and before the day is done
boxes are unpacked for the next holy day

We would crack open our own hearts
to make sure we are Hallmarked

DEFLATED

no audience, no applause
reciting Dante's Inferno
inside a balloon the size of God

deflated from too many whippets
and you in your tiny spit bubbles
shining designer shoes

solving real math equations
like who gets to remix the universal pulse
and how many bars you get to really sell that soul

'cause no one's buying tattered rags and ashes

how do we look through cracked flat screens
burning magazines
spoken word compressed to dying breath

binoculars on balcony
a sniper's cross
or a suicide note proclaimed a magnum opus

waiting for life to buffer
through scroll-down advertisements
for handbaskets full of holes

SPECTATOR SPORT

It's hard to live
when surrounded by death

hard to speak
over mass media megaphone

hard to breathe
when you don't have a mask

hard to believe
there's a god answering prayers

hard to be and not harbor seeds
of rage, distrust, dissent, disbelief

it's easy to judge
easier said than done

easy to say
"if I was there..."

It's hard to see
when eyes are clouds

throwing lightning bolts
from holy armchair in the sky

easy all-seeing
speculating from the sidelines

72

GENIUS

Such a genius.
I have all your books
upon my shelf.
You inspired me.

Once a genius.
Now all that's
left, a mess
for loved ones to mop up.

Your genius,
now chunks
and splatters
upon kitchen tiles.

SCENIC RIDE

She likes the feeling
but not the aftertaste,
chasing shots of neon lights
with orange juice flavored toothpaste

rolling fives every single time
while sixes & sevens laugh at the odds

she's like popcorn kernels
in my teeth
I like the seasoning,
I reason while my gums bleed

swallowing pints

it's OK — we survive
we like the taste

we stop breathing
just to savor air

sacrificing good veins
for a scenic ride home

when it's the same
billboards & brick & mortar
every single time

cut the taste with lime

ENVELOP

Inside
mushroom
blast radius

fallout cloud,
choosing shape
of snowflakes.

Within
verdict
raining down.

Beauty
in all things,
enveloped in tragedy.

Plucking notes
on rusted harp strings,
a universal dirge.

INCENTIVES

Street corner ad man
drafting his demise
in back alleys
black sharpie swoops
cardboard earth tones
his message, direct:
"Anything Helps"
but does it?
counting coins
measuring success
by each paper bill
incentives only
a tall can of beer
and a second-hand smoke
on this hot afternoon

CAPITAL SLUM

This city
does not inspire me

buildings degraded
people condemned

streets lined with stench
puke splattered sidewalks

this is life on the hill
where bills go to die

these times
do not define me

clothes don't fit
surroundings don't blend in

this is life in a wasteland
where rejected set up camp

they say a movement is going down
but it will take much more to move me

elephantine blocks of cynicism
occupied behind mind's picket line

PASTEL

He didn't make it,
didn't even know
what he was running from.

a lifeless carcass
just left of center divider.
what's left but fur,

and broken bones.
his misfortune,
splayed out in the road

in so much orange and red;
pastimes' pastels.
a dying breath,

a last request that next time
he may paint a picture
from the other side of street.

BALLOON

Give the boy
a blue balloon
and he'll want red

string snaps from finger,
left with
no color at all

joy floats skyward
as smile
falls to earth

grab the boy
a red balloon
now he wants green

HALFWAY TO DEVASTATED

Town square
downtown commons
look what we all
have in common

sitting on a bench
watching beautiful people
blur

while I sit here and
recoup

want to go where
we don't know
but there are too many
tourists

want to be who
we don't know
(all those beautiful
blurs)
but there's too much
at stake
(too many regrets)

listening to local talent
playing cover songs

80

corner store soothsayers
forecasting
for those not
interconnected

cornerstone fakes
crumble like cookies

rubik's cubes
and palindromes
busted drum circles
and chalk outline art

broken voices of our jaded
generation
sing in unison
counting down a chorus of
discordant days

next time we're at the same
square
let us hold hands and halt
traffic

after all
we are amateurs
in need of a few bucks

AMPUTATED

Cause is crippled
too many crutches
to lean upon

amputated whole
limbs left
to fend for selves

human kindness
compassion unraveled
like a desecrated pharaoh

hands pristine
look at what we've built
look at all we destroy

flawed clay in need of recreation

pre-approved for downfall
brakes downgrade this steep divide

kneeling at an altar of mortar & shell
machine washed and hung out to die

hands are pristine
but sculptures need some work

BUZZKILL

Seemingly serene
this scene
as I sip sunshine
thru crazy straw

dodging downward
particles
which if you let them
will ascend to
hostile takeover

a cloudless sky
turns to burst
of looming black emotion

a crying trajectory of me and you

be it nerves
or time & space
how quickly moods change
like a moon with A. D. D.

declining to talk
jaws clench tight
wrapped in concertina wire

SUMMER'S STENCH

Wandering, when
flavors were robust
colors vibrant
sounds so soothing

smells rewind mixtapes
made for first crush
time travel via
peach perfume

old friend naivete
puts cigarette burns
on milestone's upholstery

young lovers
kissing at swing set
not yet ready
for momentum

smell of chlorine
in the air
not prepared
to sink stones

here we are in summer's stench
sunglasses stealing glances
of romances never meant

to be

UMBRA

Fascinated with shadows
what lurks in subconscious

afraid of thoughts
all too often unspoken

whispers & names
so forcefully forgotten

we fight in dreams
so civil in unrest

pajamas prepare us
for such out-of-body violence

counting sheep
to shear in teardrop reflections

snoring through sunsets
and falling star tragedies

reminisce the things we miss
while drowning out reality

petrified to speak
what's on our plates and on the ends of knives

NEUROSES

There are times when in the men's room,
for a split second I wonder if
I'm really in the ladies'
and I look down at the urinal
and realize that's just absurd.

Other times I'm in an elevator
going down to the lobby,
I imagine it falling and
how much damage it would cause
to my head and internal organs
from just six flights up
(or 10, if it's lunchtime),
then the door opens and we fight
each other to see who lets who go first.

Every time we leave the house
I need to personally lock the front door
or at least double check that my wife has,
even if she says yes, of course I locked it.

And every time I get in my car I check
the windows and locks like 2 or 3 times.
(I suppose if I truly had OCD I would
know the exact number, right?)
It's not like I count the number of steps
to the sub shop (103, if walking briskly)
or anything like that.

Then of course I check my car —
rear and front bumpers, doors and windows —
for dings or perhaps a parking ticket
(I know I double-checked the signs
to make sure it's not a street sweeping week)
and I always seem to find a new scratch in
the back, though I swear I've never counted 'em.

And as I'm in the bathroom for like the 10th time
today (it's important to drink plenty of water)
I wonder what the hell is wrong with me.
Where do these thoughts come from,
and why am I so socially awkward?

Maybe I don't belong on this planet,
but I must have some purpose,
some plan to carry out
before I really do get locked inside
this elevator with colleagues,
before the wires really do snap
and send us all plummeting
express to the lobby
with one last shared moment
of sealed-in panic,
bad breath (shouldn't've had
that onion bagel for breakfast)
and sweat (GODDAMN it's hot in here)
and perhaps a silent, nervous fart.

WITHIN

.

A DISTANT HUMMING

How do I look through your sight?
When my eyelids

are slowly burning.
How do you find all the time?

When my sand
is slowly sifting.

I hear a buzzing,
a distant humming

I can't sleep through.
Did you hear something?

A sweet nothing
I can't live up to.

TRAGICTORIES

Why did I ever think
I could undo
the years with tears

sorrow,
a slingshot
in reverse

how many times I've
rehearsed this in my mind

why did I ever think
I could undo
these chains with blame

shotgun aimed,
anger yields
double-barreled backfire

how many times my
pound of flesh has tipped the scales

I dream too much,
I'm losing touch
with arm's reach

we weigh our worth
with tragedies, trajectories
but all is not as seems

FLOORBOARDS

Beneath the floorboards
lies reason

truth has been buried alive
with reasons

for giving up
not giving all

pouring soul from
empty bottle, shelved

suck to the last drop
found myself inside a teardrop

cry myself to sleep
because waking life is dry

lie, a lie, a lie
too much to deny

when I find
my face on floor

I can hear
my heart beat sore

MEDITATIONS, NO. 1

This is my life
I would not trade it till its time
I have so much to hold
to offer, to discover

this setback is temporary,
will fade away;
this ship will right its course

ERRAND OF A HYMN

Errand of a hymn
stuck inside the wind
carried on a whim

will anyone hear this silent song?

or be awakened by refrain
they don't know the words
but still they sing along

KUNDALINI WATERFALLS

Standing in abandon
he looks through a window

not just to her soul
but the soul, Super Soul
supersized consciousness

despair, distant
he rides bareback
across the ridges of her back

vertebrae mountains
tenebrous caverns fill with light
her lungs are fresh air

her red blood cells
coursing through
blue rivers and streams

her hairs, towering sequoias
skin, enriched soil
giving birth to circles

he travels up her
waterfalls
like kundalini

and he can't help but think
"I've been here before"

no longer hopeless
he comes to know

it's not a window

nor a door

but a mirror

and he steps back from the ledge

BACKLIT

Relief
barely a brief
a footnote, an afterthought

not worth while
a mention
attention span deficit

beauty is backlit
through
washed-out window slats

hard to read
like black light burial
in florescent field

moroseness
floats to surface
divine drowned in sea foam slick

crudely crying petroleum tears
blotting out sunshine
with hard-ons for soft light

FIREFLY

Mind is a firefly
trapped in cement block
wings a ghost

fluttering in dried tar
searching for
that one thought

to reignite
this shopping
center, vacant

body is burnt out
neon light, crooked

letters shattered
to unintentionally
spell dirty word

boards on glass-
less windows
vertical lips laughing

famine fortunate
absorb wrongdoings
into sun's rays

corroborating evidence
stands outside the diner

MORSELS

Too many minutes tick,
adoring outward

unobtainable
sparkles
spark less

standing there
in pretty dress
admirable admiral

false prophets
reap profits
baby's candy

too many moments lost
absorbing morsels

information trinkets
doomed, destined
to mark-down bins

once cultured
dullards scramble

in a mad attempt
to clean up past
with toxic sponge

too many second chances spent as first attempts

100

ESCAPE ARTIST

Soul searches
for next place to hide body

fingerprints
wiped clean
from crime scene

mere essence transcends
DNA strands

no murder weapon found
yet spirit is bound
to repeat cliched escapes

left longing for the kill
that would forever shed these chains

PAIN KILLERS

Wish I could
write you a smile,
write your pain away
like some kind of
verbal Vicodin.

PORCELAIN CONVICTION

Heart hiccups
a tiny cup
of self-worth,

a thimble
full of
humble reproach.

Porcelain conviction;
stripped of all veneer.

FOREVER TO HORIZON

Magical cadaver
abracadabra
cavity on yr soul
eater, brush yr teeth
brush with death
brush with fleeting optimism

pious prism
refract this lack of light

carry on
yr merry way
you prankster
mixing up change
for my ferry ride
everyone knows
you will not accept
copper to cover
sleeping eyes

see you on the other side
if I choose to be there
if I choose to cross
the river, or simply
drown in my own decay

and you'll say
fine, be that way

you cannot change a broken clock

you cannot beat
a dead horse to water

my insides are thirsty
my skin is dry

please just freeze those tears
at ducts
before our eyes tape shut

forever to horizon

THE PATH

On a new path
one with less
resistance

I dare say old
and I do mean more,
changing wicked ways
to ghost stories

how to be remembered
in these hazy atmospheric
unsure times

life is so very all or nothing

it is better to have nothing
than never quite enough

gain it all, lose nothing

TRIVIAL DUSK

years have changed
yet torment stays
the same typeface
three sources
daily deadlines
palate predicts
it's all the same and will be
any which way the circle turns
trick coin, loaded die

inside this moment
hand holds down
cannot see past tomorrow's
trivial dusk

SILENT PRAYER

I pray on sticks of incense
chant words, shake out the flame
and hope for a mend

to broken bodies
shattered still life
joyrides high on fumes

secretly wishing for the cherry
to fall out and burn down
this discontented foundation

there's got to be something more
than metaphors
to describe how we feel now

can you hear
this whimper or would
that be too simple?

to be on the lending end
of a godsend, to spare a
drop of hope to despaired

there's nothing like death
to bring the living together

nothing like death
to tear the living apart

I pray on sticks of incense
as if the smoke will carry my weight
sometimes I burn my thumb and forefinger

so it hurts to place the blame
secretly I wish for the cherry to fall out
and immolate this pain

MEDITATIONS, NO. 2

Rooftop meditations;
things seem smaller
from ten stories up.

Life is
what we make it;
coming to consensus,
a conclusion,
on our own terms.

But there are always
forces,
working on the outside.
Elements
to take into consideration.

It's enough
to bring this bundle of nerves
untethered.

So I'll take
this high altitude
inhale/exhale,

and leave it at that.

SKINLESS SADHU

I want to be a Rosary
a string of Japa beads
fingered smooth

from countless prayers
Hail Marys
Maha Mantras

blessed bracelet
wrapped
around dusted carpus

of skinless sadhu
anointed necklace
tangled through vertebrae

of fossilized saints
to be
an accessory

a holy remnant
to be
a dried out lily

on the tomb of A.D. martyr
and smell as fragrant
as first bloom

COME BACK AS

Easier said than
anything
cannot be reversed

Saturday morning,
idle hands
spilling hot coffee

How to give a fuck:
not enough;
really, that's too much

Character limit;
so tired of
selling myself short

Nosebleed yet again;
snorting lies,
shedding iron truth

Buddha and Jesus;
each stand tall
on same small altar

Subtle aurora
disguised as
new euphoria

Reflection realized
in amber—
tinted filigree

Wondrous, amorphous
doll-like face;
tenebrae undone

Bats will make a prize
of you, yours;
flittering darkness

Peaceful realms at war;
at odds with
within and without

I keep my nails short,
dirt still finds
its way underneath

Come back as a cat,
softly purr
in your perfect lap

Come back as a rat,
stealing cheese
crumbs from your pantry

Come back as a babe,
start from scratch;
perfection attempts

Come back as just me;
 "one more time"
what I said last time

Come back as a fox,
stealing pets
from backyard safeguards

Come back nevermore,
quoth raven
still rap-tap-tapping

Water comforts me;
want to be
floating inside womb

Thick sheet of dust lines
my bookshelves,
and heart's countertops

Come back as a teacher,
said student
while reading ahead

Saving copper tales
to trade for
nickel fantasies

Come back, grasshopper;
mower blades
can't break your zen calm

Alone, so serene;
but what would
I do without you?

Frozen lake constraints;
dead winter
waiting for the melt

Brown eyes mesmerize;
getting lost
in her youthful gaze

LANDLOCKED

From a landlocked state
I've seen the ocean only once,
but listened many times
through Grandma's seashell.

MEDITATIONS, NO. 3

I have undone these chains;
it's how I know the pain
is real, and happiness
the same.

SHAPE

His tiny hands
just disappear in mine
I've my father's hands
thirty years behind

I will shape him
but he shapes me
so much more

BIRTH & ITS OPPOSITE

I am tired.
Tired of writing
about bones & death
& dark shadows cast across
my soul.

Did I bring this upon myself,
some self-fulfilling synonym
for prophesied fear?

I want to breathe, to write
without obstruction.

But that is not the way
the clock turns.

Birth & its opposite;
you cannot have one
without the other.

EXPLODED VERMILION

I saw a splattered creature
in the middle of the road
as I was driving to work this morning

it was either a cat or a rabbit
I really couldn't tell
it was more exploded vermilion
than distinct features & fur

and at that moment I decided to shape
this macabre imagery into a metaphor

as I drove by, steadily
not concerned about the cleanliness of my tires
I thought this creature did the best it could
with what was given, taken, earned

one final breath, explode
dead on the side of the road

a metaphor just for you, fear

EQUALIZE

Karmic demons
dragging
dug out chains

buried ages ago
pulling
present push cart

paying for it, paying forward, paying past dues
paying against principal

ascended angel
praying
to you, equalize

reconcile sins nonlinear
realize, only I

It is up to no one else

KEEPING SCORE

Days weigh
in opposites

HEAVY

one undoes
the other

tomorrow, not always
so let's make the best of moments

let's pretend we are not
keeping score

tally, tally
rally round someone's sun
or be eaten by a cold dead rock
without name

I would rather stay warm
under a blanket of causal breath
and live in that space between
inspire, expire

BUTT OUT

Wakey, wakey.

Dreams end, eyes open.

Time to feel my aches.

I want to go back
to sleep,
but there I cannot record my progress.

When did mind become so aware of body?
Can't that fucker just butt out?

Let me enjoy this brand new day.

CULL

Convulse,
I cull you to converse
in a wayward dream

not-so-subtle strings,
contrived,
attach us to the ever after

it's here I wander
in search
of questions

quizzical grievances
latched on
like linked chains

etched upon medulla,
profound marks
counting down our days

THE LESSON

Every day,
beat it into me.
You'd think I'd have
learned the lesson
by now.

Constantly reminded,
because I
constantly forget.

Unwind
this restless spine,
and unfold
this warped coil.

I need some perspective
shoveled
down
my gullet,

so that I may
swallow
true.

O MY CHILDREN

O my children
one day I will explain to you
that everyone must die

that everything you see before you now
will one day be unseen

I must decry
wrong from right
detail concepts of God
and why it is that people kill
other people

I may profess
money isn't everything
but without it
we would be out on the streets

O my children
I will explain these aches and pains
but for now I will refrain

instead, meditate on life
let's play I Spy
board games
read your favorite books
and go to parks

for now I shall do my best to enrich your minds
and nourish your souls

126

never mind that we are hitchhiking,
my ride, an '81 Buick with rust and signs of wear
never you mind that, one day, these bodies will stop
to let us off

for now, let's just enjoy the ride
and know that you are loved with my every breath

127

FOR THE AUTHOR

You must forgive me
for wrong turns
and side street shortcuts

you must admit
uncertainty of destination;
there is no final resting place

rest in peace,
knowing
you will wake up again

just like the sun
and moon and atomic clocks
keep time

you must not dwell
on your own shadow, lest
it will pull you down into hardened cement

you must accept
destruction, as certain
as your conception

you must remember,
and forget;
start a new scratch pad

but you mustn't forget:
this ash and dust
cannot contain you

you cannot be composted,
you, a host, a holy ghost;
live life love light

rest peacefully
knowing you will
awaken from this slumber.

ABOUT THE AUTHOR

Steve Shultz lives in Aurora, Colorado, with his wife and two children. He is a journalist with The Denver Post. This is his debut poetry collection. Read more of Steve's writing at fmghost.wordpress.com.

www.ingramcontent.com/pod-product-compliance
Lightning Source LLC
Chambersburg PA
CBHW051730040426
42447CB00008B/1065